THE DEVIL

HIS ORIGIN, GREATNESS AND DECADENCE.

[*Second Edition*].

FROM THE FRENCH OF THE

REVEREND ALBERT RÉVILLE, D.D.

TRANSLATOR'S PREFATORY NOTES.

ALTHOUGH the appearance of this essay in the *Revue des Deux Mondes* must have brought it under the notice of a large number of educated Englishmen, there remain not a few to whom a translation may be serviceable. Of these, there are some who regard belief in the personality of the devil as an essential of true religion; there are others who have already come to the conclusion that such belief makes faith in our Heavenly Father's perfect wisdom, and man's free-will, impossible,* and that this form of superstition not only plies the weak with unworthy motives of conduct, but is a far slighter check upon the misbehaviour of depraved persons than is commonly assumed by theologians; and there are, doubtless, some who, not having experienced in themselves, nor observed in others, its injurious effects, regard the matter with indifference.

To those who thoughtfully reject the dark belief, this interesting essay requires no comment; but among such as hold it upon "Scriptural grounds," there may be some who are not too prejudiced to bear with the trans-

---

* Martin Luther writes: "The human will is like a beast of burden. If God mounts it, it wishes and goes as God wills: if Satan mounts it, it wishes and goes as Satan wills. Nor can it choose the rider it would prefer, or betake itself to him, but it is the riders who contend for its possession."

lator while, in no carping spirit, he ventures to ask, through the following questions, whether Scripture authorizes as distinctly as it is generally supposed to do, a doctrine which reason condemns as based upon no evidence, and as a fruitful source of mischief.

Do Moses and the older Prophets appear to have so much as heard of the devil?

Is not the Old Testament *satan* a common noun, meaning an adversary, a hindering influence? (1 Chron. xxi. 1; Psalm cix. 6). Is not, for instance, the Hebrew word translated *adversary* in the narrative of Balaam (applied there to the "Angel of the Lord"), the word which is translated elsewhere Satan? (Numbers xxii. 22).

[NOTE.—As the account of the Fall (Genesis iii.) is regarded by many as containing a mention of the Devil, we may be allowed to remark (apart from any question as to whether the episode is mythical, allegorical, or a simple record of facts) that, however general may be the notion, which Milton's grand imaginings have done much towards establishing, that the serpent was an incarnation of the Evil One, there is nothing in the narrative to support it. "The serpent was more subtle than any beast of the field." What is there here to show that the woman was surprised by any extraordinary display of subtlety on the part of the serpent, or that the animal was the mere instrument of an arch-fiend? Indeed, the curse pronounced upon the serpent race is inconsistent with such a supposition. S. Paul, in referring to the temptation of Eve (2 Cor. xi. 3), says nothing of the Devil's part in it; the serpent is not even a *satan*, but simply *the serpent*.]

Did not the Jews derive many of their notions of devils and hells, so firmly held by the Pharisees of Christ's time, from their long intercourse with the Persians?

Prefatory Notes. vii

Have not our translators of the New Testament, perplexed by the ambiguity of the Greek idiom, sometimes erred by their arbitrary suppression of the Greek article? [Christ, for instance, is made to say, "Satan cometh," "Satan hath bound," "I beheld Satan," &c., instead of *the Satan*.]

Is it not open to question whether, where Christ's words seem to confirm the notion of a personal Satan, he is doing more than accommodate his language to the popular mode of expressing the power of evil?

When Christ declares that one of his disciples is a *devil*, and when he addresses another as *Satan*, does he not use the word in its sense of *adversary*; and have these expressions any value in supporting the assertion that he taught the personality of the devil?

Has not the arbitrary treatment by our New Testament translators of the Greek word *diabolos*, which signifies an accuser, a slanderer, done much towards personifying the devil? [*Ex. gr.*, S. Paul (1 Tim. iii. 11) says that the wives of deacons must not be "devils;" that (2 Tim. iii. 2, 3), in the last time men shall be "devils;" aged women (Titus ii. 3) are to be exhorted not to be "devils," &c. Here we have, in our version, "slanderers," and "false accusers;" but where the word appears to the translators to point to the orthodox devil, the specific term is arbitrarily used.]

[NOTE.—The inquiry whether the "possessed of devils" were sufferers from physical infirmities which were popularly attributed to the agency of evil spirits, deserves consideration, but is distinct from the question of the diabolarchy.]

Does the Temptation of Christ establish the personality of the devil, seeing that this episode in the life of our Lord has by many orthodox expositors of ancient and modern times been regarded as parabolical?

In the oft-quoted passage in which the "adversary, the devil," of the converts to whom S. Peter wrote, is described as "a roaring lion" (1 Peter v. 8), does not careful perusal of the context (iv. 14-19, &c.) make it clear that the sharp exercise of the Roman rule, and no hellish Tempter, is referred to?

[NOTE.—The value of carefully comparing Scripture with Scripture cannot be over-rated; but Reference Bibles not unfrequently induce such comparison as misleads the student. The passage just quoted supplies a case in point. In the book of Job, where Satan answers the question, "Whence comest thou?" by the words, "From going to and fro in the earth, and from walking up and down in it," reference will be found to the above passage in S. Peter's epistle; and, if only the personality of the devil is first admitted, the two accounts of his roaming habits will blend very readily. "He roves," Cruden writes, "full of rage, like a roaring lion, seeking to tempt, to betray, to destroy us, and involve us in guilt and wickedness." But does the Satan of the book of Job, a poem, be it remembered, of Gentile, not of Jewish origin, bear any likeness to the Devil of the orthodox? Satan, in company with other "sons," or angels, of God, appears in the presence of the Lord, and, both in questioning the integrity of Job, and in chastening him with those trials that result in his increased happiness, acts, not as the Arch Rebel, but as the diligent servant of God. Again, in the Epistle of Jude, i. 9, occurs the passage, "Yet Michael the archangel when contending with the devil he disputed about the body of Moses, durst not bring against him a railing accusation, but said, The Lord rebuke thee." We are referred from Jude to Zachariah iii. 2. Here Satan stands, it is true, with a capital S; but a glance shows that here, as in so many other instances, "an adversary" is the correct translation.]

In 1 Cor. v. 5; and in 1 Tim. i. 20, is it possible to understand by "Satan," the diabolarch?

[NOTE.—No inquiries have been suggested as to the "dragon," "Satan," "devil" of the Apocalypse, because it is well known that the most opposite views have been taken by divines as to the whole drift of the book of Revelation, while there is hardly a passage in it that has not been used to support contradictory theories; and because the canonicity of the book—regarded in the second century as a forgery of Cerinthus, omitted in the list of books of the New Testament by the Council of Laodicea, and passed over in silence by Cyril of Jerusalem, Chrysostom, Theodore of Mopsuestia, and Theodoret—is also well known to be a vexed question with biblical scholars.]

And if in the above, and in other places, it is not conceded that we should understand by *Satan* and *Devil*, the adverse power of Rome, the obstacle opposed to the spread of the Gospel by individuals within or outside the Church, physical hindrance (2 Cor. xii. 7, and 1 Thess. ii. 18), or that "law of sin" which Paul found within him,—we may still be suffered to ask:

Is there any passage in the Epistles where the dangerous endeavours of the Tempter of our race are exposed?

How is it that where the nature of temptation is set forth, as notably in the following passage, this special business of the devil is altogether ignored?

Translator's Prefatory Notes.

"Let no man say when he is tempted, I am tempted of God, for God cannot be tempted with evil, neither tempteth he any man. But every man is tempted, when he is drawn away of his own lust and enticed. Then when lust hath conceived, it bringeth forth sin, and sin when it is finished bringeth forth death."—James i. 13-15.

[NOTE.—This passage goes far to confirm the opinion of many that the serpent of the "Fall" symbolises carnal pleasure.]

Are we at all warranted in supposing an implied intervention of the devil when Christ speaks as follows? And if "false-witness" is not the "father of lies," what is?

"OUT OF THE HEART PROCEED EVIL THOUGHTS, MURDERS, ADULTERIES, FORNICATIONS, THEFTS, FALSE-WITNESS, BLASPHEMIES."—Matt. xv. 19.

H. A.

AUTHOR'S PREFACE.

THIS little book will be found to contain the substance and general plan of the two lectures I gave at Strasburg towards the close of last autumn, and the almost literal reproduction of the article published by me in the *Revue des Deux Mondes* of the 1st January, 1870. The occasional alterations that may be remarked are, perhaps, explained by the difference that naturally suggests itself between a discourse, delivered in a Protestant Church, and an article subjected to the conditions of publication imposed by such a periodical as the above, and, again, between this and a pamphlet placed before the public upon the writer's sole authority. These alterations, moreover, affect the form only of the essay, and a few details; its basis, and the development of the ideas, remain unchanged.

I would take advantage of this opportunity of thanking my Strasburg hearers for the kind interest of which they have given me so many proofs, and of which the publication of this essay is at once a result and a new mark.

A. R.

Rotterdam, January, 1870.

HISTORY OF THE DEVIL:

HIS ORIGIN, GREATNESS, AND DECADENCE.

AMONG fallen majesties whom Time, still more than sudden revolutions, has compelled to descend slowly from the thrones they occupied, there are few whose prestige has been as imposing and as prolonged as that of the king of hell, SATAN. In speaking of him, we may safely use the expression, *fallen majesty*; for those among our contemporaries who still profess belief in his existence and power, live absolutely as if they held no such belief,—we shall presently see how those lived who *did* seriously believe in the devil,—and when faith and life are no longer in harmony, we have a right to say that faith is dead. I am speaking of course, of our educated contemporaries; the rest can no longer be taken into consideration in the history of the human mind. To give a general view of the belief in a devil, with an account of its transformations and evolutions, will, we think, be interesting. It affords well-nigh a biography. An opportunity of doing this is afforded by a remarkable work for which we are indebted to a theological professor of Vienna. Notwithstanding its occasional diffuseness, Professor Roskoff's book is an encyclopædia of all that concerns the subject; and the author will not grudge us the aid we shall derive from his treasury of erudition. May the University of Vienna, invigorated by the events which have changed the face of Austria, pay the arrears she owes to European scholarship by producing such books as this!

I.

THE origin of the belief in the devil carries us back to very early times; and, as is the case with all more or less dualistic faiths,—faiths, that is, based upon the radical opposition of two supreme principles,— we must seek it in the human mind, developing itself in the bosom of a Nature whose aspect is now favourable, now hostile. There is a certain relative dualism, an antagonism of the ego and the non-ego which reveals itself from man's birth. His first breath is painful to him, for it makes him weep. To learn to eat, to walk, to speak, is a struggle to him; and, later, the work upon which his preservation depends will reproduce this perpetual struggle under other forms. When the religious sentiment awakens within him, and, at the onset, searches its object and its food in the visible creation, he finds himself face to face with phenomena which he personifies, which are, on the one hand, lovable and loved, as the aurora, and the life-sustaining vegetation, with the rain that refreshes and fertilizes it; and, on the other hand, frightful and terrible, as storm, thunder, and darkness. Hence come good gods and evil gods. As a general rule, and in virtue of that naïve egotism which alike characterizes the childhood of individuals and of peoples, the dreaded gods are more adored than the loving deities who always do good of their own accord and unasked. This way, at least, the remarks converge of all the voyagers who have closely observed those peoples of both hemispheres who retain their savage state. We need not add that their divinities have, properly speaking, no moral character. They do good or harm according to their nature; and that is all.

Herein they do but resemble their worshippers. Man, indeed, always projects his own ideal upon the divinity he adores; and, if we consider the matter carefully, it is still thus that he arrives at the possession of all he can understand of divine truth. He has always a feeling that his god is perfect; and this is the main point; but the features of that perfection are always more or less those of his ideal. Two young swine-herds in a remote province of Austria, were once asked, "What would you do if you were Napoleon?" "I," said the younger, "would always use up the whole butter pot on my bread." "And I," said the other, who no doubt thought this answer lacked poetry, "I would watch the pigs on horseback." In like manner, a Bushman, when invited by a missionary who had instilled into him some notions of morality to give a few proofs that he could distinguish between right and wrong, said, "It is wrong for another man to come and take away my wives; it is right for me to go and take his." The gods of savages are, necessarily, savage gods. They have, for the most part, frightful forms; just as their worshippers think it proper to make themselves look hideous when they go to battle, or even when they adorn themselves. The odd, the grotesque, is to them the beautiful; whatever is uncommon is mysterious; and the unknown is terrible. The poet must pardon us if we assert that the religion of peoples of this category is simply the adoration of genii or demons of bad repute. When, passing from savage peoples who live solely by hunting and fishing, we come to pastoral and, especially, to agricultural races, this adoration of evil deities is no longer so exclusive. Still, even among these the worship of the terrible gods predominates. Take by way of illustration the simple prayer of the Madagascans, who acknowledge, among many other, two creating divinities, Zamhor, the author of good things, Nyang, of evil things:—

"*O Zamhor! To thee we offer no prayers. The good god needs no asking. But we must pray to Nyang.*

Nyang must be appeased. O Nyang, bad and strong spirit, let not the thunder roar over our heads! Tell the sea to keep within its bounds! Spare, O Nyang, the ripening fruit, and dry not up the blossoming rice! Let not our women bring forth children on the accursed days. Thou reignest, and this thou knowest, over the wicked; and great is their number, O Nyang. Torment not, then, any longer, the good folk."

It would be easy to multiply the facts which show that the large place fear has in their piety compared with veneration or love, is a characteristic feature of the religion of primitive peoples. Hence come the enormous quantity of mischievous beings of a lower rank, recognized by all inferior religions, and which we meet with in the popular superstitions which adhere so pertinaciously to religions of a more exalted spiritual level. In the grand mythologies, as those of India, of Egypt, or Greece, the apparent duality of nature is reflected in the distinction between the gods of order and production, and those of destruction and disorder. The feeling that in the long run order gains the upper hand in the contest between the opposing forces of nature, inspires *myths;* thus, Indra overcomes the storm-cloud; Horus avenges his father Osiris, wickedly slain by Typhon; and Jupiter vanquishes the Titans. Brahminism, when developed, shows us Siva, the god of destruction, concentrating and arranging the elements which disturb the universe. Siva is still the most adored of the Hindoo gods. In Semitic polytheism, dualism becomes sexual; or else the sun, always the chief object of adoration, the supreme god, is conceived under two forms, one smiling, the other terrible,—Baal or Moloch.

This two-fold character of the adored divinities is no less remarkable when we study the most poetical and serene of polytheisms, that of Greece. Like all the others, it has its root in the worship of the visible world; but more than elsewhere, unless we except Egypt, the Greek gods join to their physical nature a corresponding moral physiognomy. They conquered the agents of confusion who, under the name of Titans, Giants, Typhons, threatened to disturb established order. They are, then, the invincible preservers of the established order of things; but as, after all, this regular order is far from being always in conformity with man's physical and moral good, it follows that the Greek gods have, all of them, in varying proportions, their pleasing and their sombre aspect. Phœbus Apollo, for instance, is a god of light, a civiliser, the inspirer of art, the purifier of the earth and of the soul; and yet, he sends also plague, he is pitiless in his vengeance, and it is not very prudent to form close friendships with him. The same may be said of his sister Diana, or, rather, of the moon, who appears now with the charming features of a fair and chaste virgin, now with the sinister physiognomy of Hecate, of Brimo, or of Empusia. The azure horizons of the sea are at first beautiful blue birds; then, sea-maidens, of surpassing beauty to the waist, who bewitch navigators by their sweet love-songs: but woe to those who allow themselves to be seduced! This physiognomy, in which good and evil are mingled, is a common feature of the Hellenic pantheon, and reproduces itself unfailingly, from the supreme pair, Jupiter and Here (Juno), to the wedded occupants of the lower world, Ædoneus or Pluto, and his wife Proserpina, the *strangler*.

Like reflections are suggested by the Latin mythology; and, where original, this is even more dualistic than the polytheism of Greece. It has its Orcus, its Stryges, its Lares and Lemures. The Sclavonic mythology has its white and its black god. The divinities of our Keltic forefathers were by no means attractive, and the Germano-Scandinavian gods possessed valuable qualities allied with faults which made all intercourse with them very awkward, to say the least. Wherever in our own day belief in brownies, white-ladies, fairies, goblins, sprites, and the like has survived, we find the same admixture of good and evil qualities. These fragments of the great divine host of olden times are at once graceful, attractive, and generous, when they are in the mood; but also capricious, spiteful, and dangerous. We must keep this distinctly before us in entering upon an inquiry into the origin of our devil; for we shall find that he is of the composite order, and that many of his essential features connect him with the sombre elements of all the religions which preceded Christianity.

But there is among those religions one which, from this special point of view, deserves that we ponder awhile over its fundamental doctrines, namely, that of the Zend Avesta, or, in more common parlance, the Persian religion. For here it is that we see the divine hierarchy and creeds under the sway of a systematic dualism which extends over the whole world, including moral evil. The gods of light and the gods of darkness divide time and space between them. We do not speak here of Zarvan-Akarana, the Endless Time who gave birth to Ahuramazd, or Ormuzd, the good god, and to his brother Angramainju, or Ahriman, the god of evil; for this is a philosophical notion of much later date than that original and characteristic point of view of the Zend religion which simply recognizes two equally eternal powers which are constantly struggling together, and which meet in combat on the surface of the earth as well as in the hearts of men. Wherever Ormuzd plants good, Ahriman sows evil. The history of the moral fall of the earliest men, due to the treachery of Ahriman, under the form of a serpent, presents the most surprising analogies with the parallel account given in Genesis. Hence the assertion that the tale is merely borrowed from the Persian. I think this opinion is ill-founded, for in the Iranian myth the evil genius is disguised, while in the Hebrew account it is a genuine serpent that speaks and acts, and who involves his race in the punishment he entails upon himself. We must, then, concede to the latter history the advantage of greater antiquity, if not as to its actual form, at least with regard to its original idea. The substituting a god in disguise for an animal that reasons and speaks, points to a *reflection* unknown in the ages that gave to myths their earliest form. Such reflection, in later times, led the Jews to see their Satan under the features of the serpent of Genesis, although the canonical text by no means countenances such a supposition. I prefer, therefore, to regard the two myths, Hebrew and Iranian, as two unequally ancient variations of one and the same primitive theme, traceable, possibly, to the times when Iranians and Semitics still lived together under the shade of Ararat.

However this may be, one thing remains clear, that in the most seriously moral polytheism of the old world we meet with a religious conception which approaches very nearly to that which Semitic monotheism has handed down to us under the name of the *devil* or *Satan*. Ahriman, like Satan, has his legions of bad angels, whose only thought is to torment and ruin mortals. It is not solely physical ills, storms, darkness, floods, diseases and death, that are attributed to them, but bad desires and sinful deeds. The good man is, therefore, a soldier of Ormuzd, fighting under his command against the powers of evil; while the wicked man is a servant and, at last, an instrument of Ahriman. The Zend doctrine taught that at last Ahriman would be overcome, and would even be a convert to good. This trait distinguishes him advantageously from his Jewish-Christian brother. But here again we may ask in how far this fair hope formed part of the primitive religion.* Certain it is that there is a very close likeness between the Jewish Satan and the Persian Ahriman; and in this there is nothing strange, if we bear in mind that the Persians are the sole polytheistic people with whom the Jews, emancipated by them from the Chaldean bondage, maintained a long and friendly intercourse.

---

* There were some among Christian theologians, Origen, for instance, who believed in the final conversion of **Satan**.

Still, we must dissent from the wide-spread opinion which sees in Satan a transplanting of the Persian Ahriman into the religious soil of Semiticism. It is true that the Jewish, as well as the Christian, devil owes much to Ahriman. From the moment when the Jewish Satan makes his acquaintance, he imitates him, adopts his methods, his conduct and his tactics, and forms his infernal court upon the same pattern: in a word, he transforms himself into his likeness. But ere this, obscure and ill-defined as was his life, Satan existed. Let us endeavour to sum up his history as traced in the Old Testament.

The Israelites, and this is now clearly demonstrated, in common with other Semitic peoples, long believed in the plurality of gods; and the dualism which is at the bottom of all polytheisms has, as a necessary consequence, re-appeared among them under the forms peculiar to the ethnic group to which they belong. In proportion as the worship of Jehovah became more and more exclusive, this dualism changed its forms. The fervent worshipper of Jehovah, while he still believed in the real existence of the neighbouring deities, such as Baal and Moloch, could not but regard these immoral, cruel, and hostile gods with much the same eye as was turned upon the demons of a later age. We may go so far as to suspect some *débris* of a primitive dualism, or of an antagonism between two once rival gods, in that enigmatical being, the despair of exegetists, who, under the name of *Azazel*, haunts the desert, and to whom, on the day of atonement, the high priest sends a goat on whose head he has laid the sins of the people. But we must add, that in historic times the meaning of this ceremony seems to have been lost to those who performed it; and that, in truth, nothing can be more in opposition to anything like dualism than the Jehovistic point of view in all its strictness. With the exception of the books of Job, Zechariah, and Chronicles, all three of which are among the least ancient of the sacred collection, not a word is said about Satan in the Old Testament, not even —and this we repeat because in spite of the evidence of the text, the mistake we point out is so common—not even in Genesis. Jehovah, when once adored as the one true god, has not, could not have, a rival. Nothing happens, nothing is done on earth, which is not subject to his will; and more than one Hebrew author attributes to him directly, without the least reservation, the suggestion of errors and faults that are afterwards referred to Satan. Jehovah hardens those whom he will harden; Jehovah destroys those whom he chooses to destroy; and no one has a right to question his justice. But, as he was believed to be supremely just, it was admitted that in hardening the heart of the wicked, he did so that they might dig their own graves; while in distributing according to his will good and evil, he did so in such sort as to reward the righteous and punish wrong-doers. It was impossible to adhere constantly to this notion, so convenient in theory, but so often belied by experience; but it was long held, and a proof of this will be seen in the kind of religious ideas out of which we shall see Satan come forth.

Hebrew monotheism did not exclude belief in heavenly spirits, in *sons of God* (*beni Elohim*), in angels whose office it was to surround the throne of the Eternal, like a holy guard.* They awaited his orders, performed his will, and were in some sort the agents of divine government. Upon them devolved the direct application of the punishments and mercies of God. Consequently, there were among them some whose offices inspired fear rather than confidence. We find, for instance, an angelic

---

* Nor did it exclude the oriental belief in spirits of darkness, a kind of Djinns spoken of in Isaiah and Jeremiah, and whose character was harmful rather than otherwise. Still, anything like adoration of these gloomy genii was forbidden. A female demon of this kind called by Isaiah Lilith, the nocturnal, served in later times as a pretext for a host of Rabbinical fancies. They made of her a wife of Satan and a temptress of Adam.

messenger punishing Saul for his misdeeds, by troubling
him with dark fancies which David's harp alone can dissipate. It is an angel of the Eternal who appears with
a naked sword in his hand to Balaam, as if ready to pierce
him through, or who destroys in one night a whole
Assyrian army. In course of time an angel was distinguished among the rest whose special function in the
heavenly court was that of *accuser* of men, and whom
we might regard as the personification of a guilty conscience. Sovereign justice doubtless decided alone, and
in the fulness of its power; but not until after some
adverse debate. Now, he whose profession it was to
prosecute men at the divine tribunal was an angel whose
name *Satan* simply means *adversary*, in both the legal
and proper sense of the word. Such is clearly the Satan
of the Book of Job; he is a member of the heavenly
court, and is one of the *sons of God*, although it is his
special concern to accuse men. He has become so suspicious through his constant practice as public prosecutor,
that he believes in no human being's goodness, not even
in that of Job the just; and supposes the purest manifestations of piety to result from interested motives. We
see the character of this angel begin to tarnish; and
the history of Job shows that when his purpose is to
exhaust the resignation of a just man, he spares nothing
to effect it. It is again as the accuser of Israel that
Satan appears in the vision of Zechariah (iii. 1). This
special character of his, together with the settled belief
that angels took part in human affairs, caused Satan,
unaided by any help from Ahriman, to be feared by the
Israelites as the worst enemy of mankind; and a tendency arose, under both public and private misfortunes,
to suspect his evil agency. It resulted from this that
those fatal inspirations which earlier Jehovism attributed
immediately to Jehovah himself, came to be regarded as
proceeding from Satan. In the history of David we
have a curious instance of this evolution of religious
belief. David one day was possessed by the unlucky,

and—to the theocratic republicanism of the prophets of his time—impious idea of numbering his people. In the second book of Samuel (xxiv. 1) we are told that "the anger of the Lord was kindled against Israel, and he moved David" to give the necessary orders for this census; while, on the other hand, where the self-same history is related in the first book of Chronicles (xxi. 1), we have these words :—" And Satan stood up against Israel and provoked David to number Israel." Nothing could show better than these parallel passages the change that had come about during the interval between the composition of these two books. From this time forward the monotheist will attribute to the *Adversary* the evil thoughts and the calamities which in former times would have been traced directly to God. We may even presume that this solution of certain problems that had begun to trouble him carried with it some religious comfort; for in proportion as our conception of God becomes more elevated, it becomes harder to rest content with the childish theories that satisfied less thoughtful ages.

In the part of *adversary* of mankind, of mar-plot, we find the true origin of the Jewish and Christian devil. We must not, therefore, identify him too readily with the more or less wicked divinities of polytheistic religions. That he has *affinities* with them which grow closes and closer, we admit fully; but the certificate of his birth is clearly written ; and if even the Jews had never come into contact with the Persians, Jewish tradition would still have given us a fully-equipped Satan. Satan, then, is neither the son nor even the brother of Ahriman ; but a time came when the resemblance was so great, that it was easy to confuse them. We may say, in short, that while Ahriman is physical evil that has become moral evil also, Satan is moral evil becoming physical evil. This is the secret of his increasiug sway.

Indeed, in the so-called *apocryphal* books of the Old Testament, distinguishable from the canonical books of the same volume by the Alexandrine and Persian elements which they contain, Satan is seen growing in importance and influence. The Seventy, in translating his name by *diabolos,* from whence comes our word *devil,* retain the exact definition of his early character of *accuser.* But he comes to be something very different from that. He is an *agent provocateur* of the highest order; a very exalted personage, who, jealous to rise to a still loftier eminence among angels of the highest rank, was banished from heaven with the other spirits who were his accomplices in ambition. To hatred of men he now adds hatred of God; and it is here that the imitation of Ahriman begins. Like the Persian demon, he is at the head of an army of evil beings who execute his orders. Many of these we know by name. Among others is Asmodeus, the demon of pleasure, who plays an important part in the book of Tobit, and whose Persian origin has been rendered unquestionable by the learned researches of M. Michel Bréal. In consequence of his growing importance and his absolute separation from the faithful angels, Satan has a distinct kingdom, and a residence in the subterranean hell. Like the Persian Ahriman, he sought to spoil the work of creation, and waged war on men, whose innocent happiness was insupportable to him. And then it is agreed that he it was who, like Adam, beguiled the first woman under the guise of the serpent. It was he who introduced death with all its horrors; and hence his most formidable antagonists are those who through their great holiness are able to warn their fellows against his insidious attacks. A multitude of diseases, those especially which through their singularity and the absence of external symptoms defied natural explanations, as madness, epilepsy, St. Vitus's dance, dumbness, certain forms of blindness, &c., were attributed to his agents. Millions of fiends, obedient to his commands, were supposed to stream constantly from the depths of hell, and—like the night demons of the old faith—preferred for their haunts deserts and wildernesses. But there they grew weary, they were thirsty, they wandered about and found no rest; and their great resource was to take up their abode in a human body, that they might absorb its substance and refresh themselves with its blood. Sometimes many of them would occupy the same frame. Hence the *demoniacs* and the *possessed* of whom we read so often in the gospel narrative. Still, the Jewish mythology did not press to the utmost this likeness to Ahriman. Satan never wages war directly upon God. Certain formulas, in which the name of the Most Holy is the chief, sufficed to exorcise, to drive away, him and his angels. His power was strictly limited to the circle which it had pleased the divine wisdom to trace; so that the dualism remained very incomplete. But, for the Jewish Satan, no conversion was considered possible. As Prince of incurable evil, and knowing that the divine decrees doomed him to a final and irremediable defeat, it was held that he would persist in wickedness, and serve as executioner to supreme justice by tormenting for ever those whom he had drawn into his dreadful toils.

Such was the feeling on this head among the Jewish people when the gospel was first preached. The development of the Messianic ideas did much towards enriching the popular faith. If, as they believed, the devil dared not encounter God himself, nor even the highest of his angels, still he did not fear to resist openly his servants on the earth. Now the Messiah was to be the servant of God *par excellence*. He was to appear in order to establish the kingdom of God among the human race, which was almost wholly in the power of the devil and his angels; so that Satan would defend his dominions to the utmost against the Messiah, whose work might be summed up as consisting in a close and victorious struggle with the "prince of this world." This point of view we must never allow to escape us in our study of the gospels. Satan and the Messiah personified, on either hand, the power of evil and the power of good, ghting over every contested point a battle in which no quarter was given. Never, therefore, could Jesus have passed for the Messiah in the eyes of his countrymen, if he had not been accounted stronger than the evil spirits, whenever those *possessed* were brought to him.

Modern theology, which has well-nigh repudiated the devil, has dwelt much upon the question whether Jesus himself shared the belief of his contemporaries in regard to satanism. To treat this question adequately, it would be necessary to enter upon inquiries which are foreign to the history of the devil. We will simply remark that there is no authority for thinking that Jesus, out of consideration for popular beliefs, would have feigned a faith which he did not hold; to which we would add, that the principles of his religion were not in themselves favourable to this kind of faith. The idea that God is the Father of all, is not easily reconciled with the existence of a devil. Nowhere does Jesus make belief in the devil one of the conditions of admission into the Kingdom of God; and were the devil a mere idea, a bare symbol, these considerations would remain literally the same. Purity of heart, thirst for justice, love for God and man, these are all of them essentials which are entirely independent of the question whether Satan exists or not. So that, whenever Jesus speaks in a general, abstract sense, without regard to the circumstances of time and place, he removes the person of Satan from his field of instruction. He declares, for instance, that our evil thoughts come from our heart; while, according to the satanic theory, they ought to be referred to the devil. Still, he evidently availed himself of the popular belief on this head, as a form or image to which he attributed no positive reality. It furnished him with matter for parable. He addressed as *Satan*, one of his disciples who sought to withdraw him from approaching sufferings, and who, through very affection, became a momentary tempter. A like observation suggests itself in studying the theology of St. Paul—at least, in his authentic epistles. St. Paul evidently believes in the devil; and yet with him moral evil is connected with the earthly nature of man, and not with the external and personal action of the fiend. In a word, the teaching of Jesus and Paul does not anywhere combat the belief in the devil; but it can do without, and tends to do without it. In our own day we see abundance of good Christians who do not at all concern themselves about the king of hell; but this belief was one of those germs (of which the Gospel contains many) which required another intellectual atmosphere for their development. What precedes has explained to us why there is so much more about the devil in the New than in the Old Testament. The belief in the devil and the expectation of the Messiah had a parallel growth. Be it remarked, however, that if the New Testament often speaks of Satan and his angels, of spirits "of the air," and of the devil, "*quærens quem devoret*," its descriptions of them are almost colourless. A kind of spiritual reserve still veils all conceptions of this order. The devils are invisible; no palpable body is attributed to them; and a multitude of superstitions which will grow out of the idea that they can be seen and handled, are as yet unknown. Nevertheless, from this point of our history we may consider the origin of Satan as closed. We see him here as the link that connects polytheistic dualism with just that degree of relative dualism which Jewish monotheism could support. We are now to see him develop himself under new forms; but he has already attained a shape which we can no longer ignore. He stands before us the old Satanas, the bugbear of our forefathers, in whom is centred all that is unholy and frightful and lying—in a word, he is the ideal of *evil*.

II.

THE earliest ages of Christianity, far from developing that side of the Gospel which tended to banish the devil to the regions of symbolism and personal uselessness, served to extend his dominion, by multiplying his interventions in human affairs. He served as a scape-goat upon which the first Christians could expend their horror of heathen institutions. For some time Christians did not draw a very distinct line between the Roman Empire and the empire of Satan. This essentially Jewish point of view did not last long; but the favourite theme of most apologists was to attribute whatever polytheism presented, whether fair or foul, good or bad, to the devil's cunning and pride. Wherever the beautiful and the good were found united, this, in their eyes, was neither more nor less than so much truth artfully mixed by the enemy of mankind with fearful error, in order to retain a better grasp upon man, who could not be held under the sway of sheer falsehood. The Alexandrian school alone was more reasonable; but it had little hold upon the mass of the faithful. And now the idea spread that Satan was at bottom but a ridiculous, though for long a powerful, rival of the one adorable God. Led by a thirst for honour and dominion, he had aped, as well as he could, the divine perfections, but had only succeeded in producing a hateful caricature. But, such as it was, the caricature had blinded the nations. This subject suggested to Tertullian one of those characteristic sayings in which his satirical temper delighted: "Satan," said he, "is God's ape;" and the saying lived. The Græco-Roman gods became to Christians, as well as to Jews, demons who had usurped divine rank. The licentiousness of pagan customs, too often consecrated by traditional religious ceremonies furnished a sort of popular justification to this view which was heightened by the moral superiority which the early Church had, generally, a fair right to contrast with the corruptions that surrounded her. Satan, therefore, became, more than ever, the "prince of this world."

But let us not forget one very important circumstance, namely, that other currents external to the Christian Church contributed to spread abroad the belief in evil spirits. Polytheism in its decline obeyed its true nature; it became more and more dual. Its latest forms, those for instance which were marked by what they derived from Platonism and Pythagorism, were all saturated with dualism, and thus opened a large field to the imagination for the creation of every kind of evil genius. At that epoch, asceticism, which consists in slowly killing the body under the pretext of developing the soul, was not peculiar to the most exalted members of the Christian Church, but was found wherever a religious morality was practised. The ecstacies which were physiologically generated by fasting, gave all the appearance of reality to the imaginary beings they evoked. Apollonius of Tyana drove away as many foul spirits as a Christian saint. As Professor Roskoff very justly observes, the doctrine of angels and devils presented to both Jewish polytheism and Christian monotheism a sort of neutral territory on which, to a certain point, they could meet. The religious movements known under the name of gnostic sects, which represent, in various proportions, a mixture of heathen, Jewish, and Christian views, have as a common feature the belief in fallen angels who are the tyrants of men and the rivals of God. The great success of Manicheism, that confluence of Persian dualism and Christianity, is due to the leaning of public opinion towards whatever portrayed a systematic struggle between the genius of evil and the genius of good. The Talmud and the Kabbala were subjected to the same influence. We must not regard Christianity as alone responsible for the prominent place Satan took in the concerns of this world; it was a universal tendency of the epoch, and we should be more correct in regarding Christianity as affected thereby in common with all other contemporaneous forms of religion.

The Jewish Messiah became to Christians the Saviour of guilty humanity. This is why we see the radical antagonism between Satan and the Messiah reflected in the primitive doctrine of redemption. From the close of the second century, this doctrine is summed up in a grand drama in which Christ and the devil are the principal actors. The multitude were contented to believe that Christ, descending into hell, had, in virtue of his right as the stronger of the two, taken from Satan the souls he had carried captive. But this rude idea underwent a refinement. Irenæus taught that man, after the fall, having become Satan's rightful property, it would have been unjust on the part of God to deprive him by violence of his own; and that Christ, as a perfect man, and therefore independent of the devil, offered himself a ransom for the human family, which bargain the devil accepted. Soon, however, it became clear that the devil had made a very foolish reckoning, as Christ did not remain, after all, in his power. Origen, whose ecclesiastical teachings must not always be taken as literally exact representations of his real opinions, became the organ of views which freely admitted that both Christ and Satan had played their parts very cleverly, seeing that the devil believed he should keep in his power a prey which was worth more to him than the whole human race, while Christ knew very well that he should not remain in Satan's hands. This view, which made Jesus the deceiver at the cost of Satan, scandalous as it appears to us, was, nevertheless, a success, and long predominated in the Church. Ecclesiastical poetry, popular preaching, and even pontifical assertion, extended it in all directions, dramatised it, consecrated it. One can readily understand that this way of regarding redemption did not go towards diminishing the devil's sway over men's minds. Nothing did more to increase fear of the enemy than vague descriptions of the immensity of his power, and of the risk run by exposure to his attacks; especially as, by a singular contradiction from which the ancient theology never succeeded in extricating itself, the devil, although declared vanquished, overthrown, and rendered powerless by his victor Christ, did not the less maintain his infernal sway over a large majority of mankind. The saints alone could count themselves safe from his ambushes; and, according to the legends which now began to spread, great was the prudence and energy they required to escape him! Everything turned upon this constant state of watchfulness. Baptism dwindled into an exorcism. To become a Christian, was to renounce the devil with his pomps and works. Expulsion from the fold of the Church, whether for immoral behaviour, or for heterodoxy, was the being "delivered over to Satan." It was thus that during this period the doctrine of the fall of the evil angels was developed. We now find it taught that devils were referred to in that mythic passage of Genesis where the "sons of God saw the daughters of men that they were fair, and took them wives of all that they chose," licentiousness being considered as the original sin and never-ending concern of evil spirits; and again, as this hypothesis did not explain the anterior presence of a wicked angel in the earthly paradise, the fall of the rebel fiends was dated from the moment of the Creation. Augustine thought that in consequence of this fall, their bodies, which were formerly subtle and invisible, became dense. And here we have the beginning of a belief in the visible apparitions of the devil. Then came another notion, that devils, in order to gratify their lust, took advantage of the night to surprise young persons while asleep; and hence the *succubæ* and *incubi* which played such a prominent part in the middle ages. Saint Victor, according to the legend, was overcome by a demon who had artfully assumed the form of a young seductress who had lost her way at night time in the woods. The councils, from the fourth century, enjoined bishops to keep a close watch over those in their dioceses who practised magic arts, the inventions of the devil; and wicked women are spoken of who are supposed to run the fields by night in the train of Diana and other heathen goddesses. But as yet these imaginary *sabbaths* are regarded as but dreams suggested by Satan to those whose vicious inclinations gave him a hold over them.

Ere long, however, all became real and material. There was not a saint to whom the devil did not at least appear once under a human form. Saint Martin even met him so disguised as to represent Christ. For the most part, however, in his quality of angel of darkness, he appeared as a man, and quite black, under which colour he was wont to escape from the heathen temples and idols that had been thrown down by the zeal of converts to the new religion. And then came the idea that one could make an agreement with the devil, by which the soul might be exchanged for the object of one's greatest desire. This notion dates from the legend of Theophilus, a sixth century saint. He, in a moment of wounded pride, made himself over formally to Satan; but, being devoured by remorse, he got the Virgin Mary to recover the fatal document from the evil one.*

This legendary episode, written with the express object of extending the worship of Mary, necessarily had important results. The devil, moreover, saw his prestige increase still further, when the conversion of the

---

* The *Golden Legend* of Jacobus de Voragine teaches us why Satan was not content to take a simple verbal promise. "The Christians," said he, "are cheats; they make all sorts of promises as long as they want me, and then leave me in the lurch and reconcile themselves with Christ as soon as, by my help, they have got what they want."

invaders of the Empire, and the missions sent into countries that had never formed part of the Roman dominions, introduced into the bosom of the Church a mass of grossly ignorant people, who were still impregnated with polytheism. The Church and State, which had been united since Constantine's time, and were still more closely cemented under Charlemagne, did what they could to refine the coarse minds of those whose teachers they had become; but, to do this effectually, the temporal and spiritual powers had need to be themselves less under the sway of the very superstitions they desired to repel. If some among the more clever of the Popes succeeded in combining with their political plans a certain amount of toleration for customs and errors that seemed ineradicable, the great majority of bishops and missionaries firmly believed that by insisting upon the extirpation of polytheism they were fighting against the devil and his host. They inoculated their converts with the same belief; and thereby considerably prolonged the existence of the heathen divinities. The good old rural spirits died hard. The sacred legends contain many of them, and comparative mythology recognises not a few ancient Keltic and Teutonic gods among the patron saints of our ancestors. Saint Nicolas, Saint Victor, Saint Denis with the "head-carrying" saints in general, Saint Ursula (Horsela), Saint Venetia, and many others of less fame, enter into this category. For a long time, and without its being looked upon as a renunciation of the catholic faith, it was usual in England, France, and Germany, to offer presents, now out of gratitude, now through fear, to the spirits of the fields and forests,—women especially adhering to such old customs. But as the Church still regarded as demons and devils all superhuman beings who were not saints or angels, seeing that the character of the old gods had nothing angelical in it, an interchange, or, rather a transformation, was effected. The good side of these deities served, under new names, to enrich the kingdom of the saints, the kingdom of the demons had what was left. Belief in the devil, which in the earlier ages had something elevated in it, became simply gross and stupid. At the beginning of the middle ages certain animals, as cats, toads, rats, mice, black dogs, wolves, were regarded as specially selected by the devil and his servants for symbols, auxiliaries, and even as temporary disguises. In our own times even, we generally find these animals were consecrated or sacrificed to the divinities whom demons have replaced. Traditions of human sacrifices offered up in honour of the ancient gods, account doubtless for the notion that Satan and his slaves have a relish for human flesh. The were-wolf who eats children has been by turns a god, a devil, and a sorcerer who went to the *sabbath* under the guise of a wolf that he might not be recognised. We all know that there is no witch without her cat. Vermin, that sore which then as now was but too common a scourge among populations devoid of all sense of cleanliness, was also to be laid at the door of the devil and his servants.* A time came when the idea

---

* Nearly twenty years ago, while labouring as a pastor in a village in the north of France, I was sent for by a poor and ignorant workman, who was living with his wife and six children in the greatest misery. His household was in the most wretched state, being infested with vermin which it seemed impossible to get rid of. Every one, the poor people feared, would soon hear of their state, and refuse them work. A *liard*—liards were still in circulation—that had been seen *to move alone*, had, they firmly believed, brought them their bad luck; and the sorcerer, they were no less sure, was a neighbour who bore them a grudge. I had all the trouble in the world in keeping the father of the family from avenging himself upon the supposed sorcerer, whom he wished to throttle, and in persuading him to take a note I gave him to the village apothecary; nor did *I* succeed in driving from his head the notion that the liard which "went alone" had to do with his misfortune. On picking up from under an article of furniture the dreadful liard which he dared not touch, and bringing it to him to show there was nothing to fear, he said, "It's all very well for *you*, Sir; you understand Latin." Understanding Latin was to those poor folk what "reading the runes" was among the old Scandinavians. How many such scenes must have been enacted during the middle ages, when the clergy, far from opposing such absurdities, were themselves but too ready to believe in them!

that the devil had a distinct bodily shape became settled; and this form was that of the ancient fauns and satyrs, with horns, protruding legs, hairy skin, tail, cloven foot or horse's hoof.

It would be easy to accumulate here semi-burlesque, semi-tragic details. But we prefer marking the salient points of the development of belief. We have reached a period at which we must look at it under a new light. Among the Jews of the times immediately preceding the Christian era, Satan had become the *adversary* of the Messiah; with the early Christians he was the direct antagonist of the Saviour of mankind: but to the middle ages Christ was up in heaven, far away; and the immediate, living organism in which his kingdom on earth was to be realised was the Church, between which and the devil the war was thenceforward to be waged. The faith of the peasant consists simply in believing what the Church believes. Ask him what the Church believes, and he will answer boldly, "What I believe." And if in the times of which we are speaking the question had been put, "What does the devil do?" the answer would have been, "What the Church does not do;" while to the question, "And what is it that the Church does not do?" the response would have amounted to this, "What the devil does." The *sabbaths* which the ancient councils, when referred to thereupon, treated as appertaining to imaginary regions, had now been something very real. The Germanic idea of *fealty*, the idea that fidelity to the suzerain was the first of virtues, just as treason on the par of the vassal was the greatest of crimes, was introduced into the Church, and contributed not a little to give to aught approaching infidelity to Christ the colour of the blackest depravity. The wizard was as faithful to his master the devil as was the good Christian to his heavenly liege; and just as vassals came yearly to render homage to their lord, so did the feudal servants of Satan hasten to pay him like honour, either on some accustomed day or at a special convocation. The weird chase through the air of wizards and witches, as they hastened to the nightly rendezvous, was no other than a transformation of the Keltic and German myth of the *Wild Huntsman*. But the master who awaited them was a sort of god; and in the grand assemblies of the devilish horde he was honoured by the celebration of a burlesque of the mass; the spirit of evil being worshipped by reversing the ceremonies which serve to glorify the author of good. The very name of *sabbath* came from the confusion of devil-worship and mere non-catholic rites; the Church having placed on the same footing Jews, excommunicate persons, heretics, and necromancers. To this confusion there was one circumstance which contributed greatly. Into most of the sects that had revolted against the Church (and above all the one which holds so exalted and so sad a place in French history, that of the *Albigenses*) the old gnostic and Manichæan leaven had thoroughly instilled itself. Dualism was the principle of their theology.* This accounts for the idea that at their religious meetings, which rivalled the mass, they simply said the mass-service backwards, a mode of worship which was in high favour with Satan. If, bearing this in mind, we remember how easily in mediæval times the State allowed itself to be persuaded that its main business was to exterminate heretics, we shall cease to wonder at the severity of the penal laws directed against supposed sorcerers.

The absorbing nature of the belief in the devil during the middle ages is the point we wish to make clear.

---

* I am, of course, speaking here of the leaders and the initiated, for the multitude could not fathom the complicated doctrine of *cantharism*. They saw in it nothing more than a violent expression of hatred of the priesthood. Thence comes another misunderstanding, not uncommon in our own days, between the Vaudois, who are free from all dualism, and the Albigenses, whose dualism was, in some sort, the official belief.

Those who have still this faith can hardly imagine to what a degree it then controlled men's whole lives. It was the one fixed idea with every one, particularly from the thirteenth to the fifteenth century, the period at which we may consider this superstition to have reached its climax. A fixed idea tends, among those whom it possesses, to centre everything in itself. When, at the present day, we observe closely those of our contemporaries who devote themselves to spiritualism, it is surprising to see how fertile their imagination becomes when they are busy in interpreting in favour of their hobby the most trifling and unimportant circumstances. The unlatching of a half-closed door, an insect describing arabeques in its flight, the fall of a badly-balanced article, the creaking of furniture at night-time, any one of these petty accidents suffices to give wing to their fancy. If we generalize such a mental state, by substituting faith in the incessant interventions of the devil for the harmless illusions of our spiritualists, we shall get a fair notion of what took place in the middle ages. Among the numberless records from which we might quote, we will take the *Revelations* of the Abbot Richalmus, who lived in Franconia some seven hundred years ago, and who belonged to the Cistercian order.* These *Revelations*, though now forgotten, had formerly a wide-spread fame. Abbot Richalmus boasted the possession of a special power of discerning and detecting the machinations of Satan's satellites, who moreover, according to the abbot, were especially given to playing their impish tricks upon churchmen and good Christians. And right diabolically did they worry the poor man! From his distraction during mass to the nausea that too often troubles his digestion, from the discords of the choir-men to the fits of coughing that interrupt his sermons, all is of fiendish agency. "For instance," says

---

* Liber Revelationum de Insidiis et Versutiis Dæmonum adversus Homines.

he to his attendant, "when I sit down to holy studies, the devils make me feel heavy with sleep. Then I stretch my hands beyond my cuffs to give them a chill. Forthwith the spirits prick me under my clothes like so many fleas, which causes me to put my hands there; and so they get warm again, and my reading grows careless." They love, he tells us, to make people ugly. To one they give a red nose, to another cracked lips. If a man likes to close his mouth decently, then they make his lower lip droop. "Come," he says to his acolyte, "just look at my lip; for twenty years has an imp clung to it, just to make it hang down." And so on, in the same strain. When asked whether there are many devils who thus wage war with man, the abbot Richalmus replies that each one of us is as closely surrounded by them as a man when plunged in the sea is by the waves. Fortunately, the sign of the cross was generally enough to disconcert them; but not always, for they understand well the human heart, and know how to take advantage of its weak side. One day, when some monks were gathering together stones under the abbot's orders, for the purpose of building a wall, he heard a young devil who was hidden under them call out very distinctly, "What a troublesome task!" This he did that he might dispose the monks to grumble at the labours imposed upon them. To the sign of the cross, he tells us, it is often useful to add the aid of holy water and salt. Evil spirits cannot bear salt. "When I am at dinner, and the devil has taken away my appetite, as soon as I have tasted a little salt it comes back to me; and if, shortly afterwards, I lose it again, I take some more salt, and am once more an hungered." Here we have the old idea that salt was preservative, vivifying, agreeable to gods and men; and, consequently, opposed to whatever is ungodly. In the hundred and thirty chapters which make up his *Revelations*, the abbot scarcely does anything but subject to his one fixed idea the most trivial events of domestic and, particularly, of convent life. But the popularity this book, which was published after his death, enjoyed, proved that he had simply abounded in the notions of his contemporaries. Innumerable parallels may be found in the literature of the age. The *Golden Legend* of Jacobus de Voragine, one of the most popular books of the middle ages, would suffice as an illustration.

This incessant turning of the thoughts devilward, had two equally logical consequences, though they were of a very opposite character. It had its comic and its serious aspect. Through seeing Satan everywhere, a familiarity with him was engendered, and by a kind of unconscious mental protestation against the imaginary monsters created by traditional teaching, people got so bold as to manage his horned majesty very easily. The legends pictured him always as so miserably outdone by the sagacity of saints and holy priests, that his reputation for cleverness gradually waned. It was thought by no means impossible to turn his stupidity to account. Had he not, for instance, been such a simpleton as to get architects out of hobbles by supplying them with splendid plans for the cathedrals of Aix-la-Chapelle and Cologne? It is true that at Aix he had bargained for the soul of the first person who entered the church, and at Cologne for that of the architect himself; but then he was outwitted, after all. At Aix, a wolf was goaded into the newly-finished church; at Cologne, the architect, having got possession of the promised plan, instead of giving Satan a proper deed by which his soul was made over, suddenly draws from under his gown a bone of one of the eleven thousand virgins, which he thrusts into the evil one's face, who makes off with a thousand oaths. It is well known how prominent was the part assigned him in the mediæval religious plays. The popular imagination still pictured the redemption as a divine stratagem by which the enemy of mankind was fairly duped; and thus it was easy to conceive a host of other cases in which Satan was caught in his own net.

What laughter his scrapes excited among the good folk! There are ample reasons for believing that he became the personage who was the most to their taste, if he did not gain the largest share of their sympathy. The rest of the *dramatis personæ* had their parts traced out for them by tradition; in his case there was always room for a little extemporaneous acting. For a long time he represented the comic element of the sacred drama. His character, half mountebank, half grim, was conveniently flexible. In France, where there has always been an inclination to subject the theatre to precise rules, there were popular pieces called *devilries*, vulgar and often obscene masquerades, in which at least four devils were expected to display their gambols, and, from which it would seem we get the expression, *faire le diable à quatre*. In Germany, too, the devil was an amusing character on the stage. There is an old Saxon "mystery" of the Passion, in which Satan repeats as a mocking echo the last words of Judas while he hangs himself; then, when according to the sacred tradition the bowels of the traitor gush out, he puts them into a basket, and sings an appropriate ditty as he carries them off.

But all this did not prevent the devil's generally causing terrible fear. To go to the play was, in the middle ages, much the same as going to church. When there, there was nothing to hinder one's making a butt of the hated being whose malice was powerless to harm the actors in the sacred performances. But listening to *mysteries* could not be made the main business of life; and the realities of every day soon restored his prestige. The number of persons who were suspected of having dealings with Satan was enormous; so great, that when the success of an enemy or of a bold plot seemed otherwise inexplicable, it was at once set down to Satanic agency. Enguerrand de Marigny, the Templars, poor Joan of Arc, and many other illustrious victims of political hatred, were convicted of witchcraft. Among the Popes themselves, some, as John XXII., Gregory VII., and Clement V., encountered the same suspicion. At this epoch the notion arose that agreements made with the devil must be signed with the blood of those in league with him, that it might be clearly understood that their persons and lives were his; while the old Italian superstition was resuscitated by which one's enemy was destroyed by mutilating or piercing little waxen figures, made in his image, and placed under a spell. Councils were summoned expressly to check the supposed spread of witchcraft. Pope John XXII., himself accused of necromancy, declared, in a bull promulgated in 1317, what bitter grief was caused him by those compacts made with the devil by his physicians and courtiers, by which other men were led to take part in the like impious doings. From the thirteenth century, the crime of sorcery was placed on a level with the greatest offences; and popular ignorance was but too ready to furnish fuel to the zeal of the inquisitors. At Toulouse a noble lady, fifty-six years of age, Angela de Labarète by name, was the first who was burned as a sorceress, in which special quality she formed part of the great auto-da-fé which took place in that city in 1275. At Carcassonne, from 1320 to 1350, more than four hundred executions for witchcraft are on record. Up to the end of the fourteenth century, however, these horrible displays were localized; but in 1484 a decree of Pope Innocent VIII. extended trial for witchcraft over the whole of Christendom. Then began in Europe that hideous witch-hunt which marks the climax of the belief in the devil, which concentrated and condensed it during more than three centuries; and which at last, succumbing to the moral force of modern times, was to carry away with it the dark belief from which it arose.

III.

IN the fifteenth century a momentary lull of orthodox fanaticism rendered the inquisitor's task somewhat difficult in the treatment of heresy proper. On the banks of the Rhine as well as in France, people seem to have begun to weary of the insatiable ghoul that threatened everybody, while it healed none of the ills of the Church to which it had been applied as a sovereign remedy. Faith in the Church itself as a perfect and infallible institution was tottering, and the inquisitors carried to the Holy See their murmurs at the increasing obstacles placed in their way by local powers and parish clergy. Still, even those whose faith in the Church was shaken, and who inclined towards religious toleration, did not propose to leave a free course to the devices of the devil and his agents. It was at this time that the famous bull *Summis desiderantes* appeared, by which Innocent VIII. added to the power of the officers of the Inquisition that of prosecuting those guilty of witchcraft, and of applying to them the rules which hitherto had only been aimed at *depravatio hæretica*. Long is the list of machinations enumerated in the pontifical bull, from tempests and the destruction of crops to the spells cast upon men and women to prevent the increase of the human family. Armed with this bull, which thundered the severest pains and penalties against the refractory, and which was confirmed by other decrees of the same sense and origin, the inquisitors Henry Institoris and Jacob Sprenger wielded that *Witch-Hammer,—Malleus Malificarum,*—which was long throughout Europe the standard code of action against those suspected of sorcery. It received the sanction of the Pope, and the approval of the Emperor Maximilian and of the theological faculty of Cologne. The perusal of this heavy and wearisome treatise can hardly fail to provoke a shudder; a careful study of the false put in the stead of the true, of the repeated sophisms with which the book abounds, of the pedantic folly with which its authors heap together whatever can give a shadow of likelihood to their nightmares, together with the cold-blooded cruelty which dictates their prosecutions and summonses,—this could not but disgust the modern student, were it not his duty to bring to the bar of history one of the most lamentable aberrations that have warped the conscience of humanity.

Everything is explained in this conjuring-book. We learn why the devil* enables his servants to change themselves *reali transformatione et essentialiter* into wolves and other dangerous animals; why it is heresy to disbelieve in the power of magic; how the *incubi* and *succubæ* work their ends: why the number of witches is greater than ever; why David in olden time drove away the spirit that troubled Saul by showing him a harp in the form of the cross, &c. We are told, again, that the reason why there are more witches than wizards lies in the fact that women are more ready than men to be beguiled by the devil's promises; and this, because the *fluidity* of their temperament makes them more easily acted upon by his inspiration; in a word, because being weaker than men they readily seek supernatural aid in order to satisfy their vengeance or their sensuality. All manner of recipes are recommended to persons who have the good sense to guard themselves against the charms that may be practised upon them. The sign of the cross, holy water, the judicious use of salt, and of the name of the Holy Trinity, are among the principal exorcisms.

---

* The authors gravely state that the word *diabolus* comes from *dia* or *duo* and *bolus, quod est morsellus,* because the devil, they say, kills two things, *scilicet corpus et animum*.

The sound of bells is accounted a very energetic preservative; and therefore it is well to ring them during storms, as the evil spirits, who cannot support the sacred sound, are thereby driven away, and checked in their work of perturbation. This superstitious custom, which has lasted to our own day, denotes clearly the confusion of demons ecclesiastic with the old divinities of storm and tempest.

But what is above all worthy of attention, is the mode of criminal action developed in this book, and which became law everywhere. It is exactly based upon the prosecutions instituted by the Inquisition against heretics. As witchcraft was the outcome of a league with the devil it presupposed the abjuration of the baptismal vow, and was, consequently, a kind of apostacy, a heresy of the gravest order. Denunciations without proof were admitted. Even public hearsay sufficed to bring the charge under the judge's scrutiny. The depositions of all comers were received, no matter how infamous, no matter whether or not they were the enemies of the accused parties. The trial was to be as summary as possible, and useless formalities cut short. The witch was to be cross-questioned until something peculiar was detected in her life that served to strengthen the suspicions which hung over her. The judge was not obliged to name her accusers. She was allowed a defender, who knew no more of the matter than she did, and who had to limit what he said to the defence of the person accused, but not of her criminal acts, as this would turn suspicion upon himself. Confession was to be obtained by torture, together with all the circumstances connected with the offence.

In order to obtain full and prompt confession, her life might be promised her; but—and this is expressed in so many words—such promise was not binding. Torture was to be repeated every three days; and the judge was to use all needful caution lest its effects should be neutralised by charms hidden about the person of the accused.

He was even to abstain from looking her in the face, seeing that witches had been known to be gifted by the devil with an influence which made judges who thus gazed on them unable to pronounce their condemnation. When at last she had been well and rightly convicted, she was to be delivered over to the secular arm, to be put to death without further parley.

This rapid glance is enough to show that the unhappy creatures who fell into the clutches of this terrible tribunal, might well leave all hope at their prison door. There is nothing more shocking than an attentive examination of witch trials. Women were always, as we have seen it learnedly explained, in the majority. Hatred, jealously, vengeance, and, more than all, suspicions caused by wretchedness and ignorance, found in these trials a vent of which they did not fail to avail themselves. Not unfrequently, poor creatures were the victims of their own imagination, stimulated by an hysterical temperament, or by the fear of hell fire. Those who in our own day have had an opportunity of examining cases of religious mania know how readily women believe themselves fallen from grace and given over to the power of the evil one. All such sad cases, which are now treated with the greatest tenderness in institutions devoted to their care, were then looked upon as "possessions" of the devil, or as witches, and, horrible to think of, not a few of them believed it themselves! Many related that they had been to the *sabbath*, and had given themselves up to the most shameful excesses. Greatly must such confessions have aggravated the danger of those who denied with the firmness of innocence that they had committed the abominations of which they were accused! Torture was at hand to tear from them what they refused to say, and thus the belief took deep root in the minds of the judges, even when they were comparatively humane and just, that over and above crimes committed by natural means, there was a long list of offences the supernatural origin of which made them doubly heinous. And how was it possible to deal too sharply with such offences?

In the single year 1485, and in the district of Worms alone, eighty-five witches were delivered to the flames. At Geneva, at Basle, at Hamburg, at Ratisbon, at Vienna, and in a multitude of other towns, there were executions of the same kind. At Hamburg, among other victims, a physician was burnt alive because he saved the life of a woman who had been given up by the midwife. In Italy, during the year 1523, there were burnt in the diocese of Como alone more than two hundred witches. This was after the new bull hurled at witchcraft by Pope Adrian VI. In Spain it was still worse; there, in 1527, two little girls of from nine to eleven years of age denounced a host of witches, whom they pretended to detect by a mark in their left eye. In England and Scotland, political influence was brought to bear upon sorcery; Mary Stuart was animated by a lively zeal against witches. In France, the Parliament of Paris happily removed business of this kind from the ecclesiastical tribunals; and under Louis XI., Charles VIII., and Louis XII. there were but few condemnations for the practice of magic; but from the time of Francis I., and especially from Henry II., the scourge re-appeared. Jean Bodin, a man of sterling worth in other respects, but stark mad upon the question of witchcraft, communicated his mania to all classes of the nation. His contemporary and disciple, Boguet, showed how that France swarmed with witches and wizards. "They increase and multiply on the land," said he, "even as do the caterpillars in our gardens. . . . . Would that they were all got together in a heap, so that a single fire might burn them all at once." In Savoy, Flanders, the Jura Mountains, Lorraine, Béarn, Provence, and in almost all parts of France, the frightful hecatombs were seen ablaze. In the seventeenth century the witch-fever somewhat abated, though it burst out here and there, centralizing itself chiefly in the convents

of hysterical nuns. The terrible histories of the priests
Gaufridy and Urban Grandier are well known. In
Germany, and particularly in its southern parts, witch-
burning was still more frequent. In one small prin-
cipality at least 242 persons were burnt between 1646
and 1651 ; and, *horribile dictu,* in the official records of
these executions we find that among those who suffered
were children of from one to six years of age! In
1657 the witch-judge, Nicholas Remy, boasted of having
burnt 900 persons in fifteen years. It would even
seem that it is to the proceedings against sorcery that
Germany owes the introduction of torture as an ordinary
mode of getting at the truth. Mr. Roskoff reproduces
a catalogue of the executions of witches and wizards
in the episcopal town of Würzburg in Bavaria, up to
the year 1629.* He enumerates thirty-one executions in
all, not counting some regarded by the compilers of the
catalogue as not important enough to mention. The
number of victims at each execution varies from two to
seven. Many are distinguished by such surnames as
*The Big Hunchback, The Sweetheart, The Bridge-keeper,
The Old Pork-woman,* &c. Among them appear people of
all sorts and conditions, actors, workmen, jugglers, town
and village maidens, rich burghers, nobles, students,
magistrates even, and a fair number of priests. Many
are simply entered as "a foreigner." Here and there is
added to the name of the condemned person, his age and
a short notice. Among the victims, for instance, of the
twentieth execution figure " Little Barbara, the prettiest
girl in Würzburg;" "a student who could speak all
manner of languages, who was an excellent musician
vocaliter et instrumentaliter ;" " the master of the hos-
pice, a very learned man." We find, too, in this gloomy
account, the cruel record of children burnt for witchcraft;

---

* In 1659 the number of those put to death for witchcraft
amounted in this diocese to 900. In the neighbouring bishoprick
of Bamberg at least 600 were burnt.

here, a little girl of about nine or ten years of age, with her baby sister, younger than herself (their mother was burnt a little while afterwards); here, boys of ten or eleven; again, a young girl of fifteen; two children from the poor-house; the little boy of a councillor . . . . The pen falls from one's hand in recapitulating such monstrosities. Cannot those who would endow catholicity with the dogma of papal infallibility hearken, before giving their vote, to the cries that rise before God, and which history re-echoes, of those poor innocent ones whom pontifical bulls threw into the flames?

The seventeenth century saw the rapid diminution of trials and tortures. In one of his good moments, Louis XIV. mitigated greatly the severity of this special legislation. For this he had to undergo the remonstrances of the parliament of Rouen, which believed society would be ruined if those who dealt in sorcery were merely condemned to perpetual confinement. The truth is, that belief in witchcraft was so wide-spread that, from time to time, even throughout the seventeenth century, there were isolated executions. One of the latest and most notorious was that of Renata Saenger, superior of the convent of Unterzell, near Würzburg (1748). At Landshut, in Bavaria, in 1756, a young girl of thirteen years was convicted of impure intercourse with the devil, and put to death. Seville, in 1781, and Glaris, in 1783, saw the last two known victims to this fatal superstition.

IV.

A WEAPON has sometimes been framed against Christianity out of these brutal deeds. It has been affirmed that they are traceable to a belief with which Christianity alone had inoculated nations who would have otherwise ignored it. This point of view is superficial, and historically inaccurate. The fault really lies at the door of dualism, which is far older than the Christianity it has outlived. Pagan antiquity had its necromancers, its magicians, its old ghoul-like *lamiœ* and *veneficœ*, who were no less feared than our witches. We have shown that dualism is inherent in all forms of nature-worship; that these "natural" religions, when at their full development, result, as in Persia, in India, and even in the latest evolutions of Græco-Roman paganism, in an eminently dualistic conception of the forces or divinities which direct the course of events:—that the Jewish Satan owes, not his personal origin, but his growth and total depravity, to his contact with the Persian Ahriman: and that the Satan of the Christians inherited in his turn, and his angels with him, the worst side of the character of the vanquished divinities, together with the most frightful of their symbolisms. Indeed, the devil of the middle ages is at once heathen, Jewish and Christian. He is Jewish and Christian, because moral evil is his proper domain; for the physical evils of which he is the author arise solely out of his eager desire to corrupt men's souls, which, for their part, only give themselves up to him for criminal purposes: and he is so inasmuch as his power, great as it may be, cannot transcend the boundaries it has pleased divine authority to mark out. He is heathen in all that he retains of the old polytheistic belief. The *medieval* faith in demons may be regarded as paganism taking its "revenge," or as the non-absorbed residuum of polytheism, perpetuating itself under new forms.

It was not solely the authority of the Church that prolonged the reign of Satan and his angels; it was mainly the intellectual condition which is betrayed, up to an epoch approaching our own, by all works of any scientific pretension during the whole period anterior to Bacon and Descartes. Anything like real knowledge of nature did not exist; that her laws were inviolable, had yet to be declared. Alchemy, astrology, and the medical practice of the time, all turned upon magic; they, no less than the theology of the age, were based upon belief in occult influences, in talismans, in the power of words, and in impossible transmutations. Even after the Renaissance, what a mystic and superstitious medley is presented in the physiological doctrines of Cardan and Paracelsus and Van Helmont! The general state of men's minds, determined, I acknowledge, to a great extent by the Church, but by the Church while herself undergoing the influence of preponderating ideas—has been the real cause of that long series of follies and abominations which constitutes the history of the devil in the middle ages and in modern times. The proof of this may be seen in the fact that, at a time and in countries where the Church was still very powerful and by no means lenient, the belief in the devil gradually faded out of real life, suffered repeated attacks, and at last fell into ridicule without such a grave change in the ideas of enlightened Europe being signalised by any remarkable persecution. The imagination of the ages of ignorance sometimes takes a prophetic flight. The old writer tells us how that at the hour of night appointed by the king of hell for the *sabbath* of his faithful followers, demons, witches, and wizards assemble from all parts of the rendezvous. The place of meeting is generally a waste heath, a forest glade, or a naked mountain-top. They come from every quarter of the horizon, breathless, dishevelled, frenzied. Scarcely have they alighted, ere they turn towards Satan to pay him their dismal homage. He contemplates with pride the great army of the accursed. They are his, body and soul. The wind moans as it passes over the hellish gang. The moon scarcely dares to peer through the dark fringes of the heavy clouds. Bats, owls, ospreys hover in its pale rays. Soon the sacrilegious ceremony ends, and the orgies begin: nameless dances, contortions, yells, the blasphemies of the damned,—a deafening rout! Woe to the benighted wanderer who becomes the unwilling witness of these hideous revelries! .... But suddenly a low but clear sound is heard. It is the crow of a cock in the neighbouring village. A ray of light silvers the horizon. With it, everything vanishes; every vestige of the whirling throng is gone. The very grass shows no trace of the footsteps of the gang. What has happened? .... The old writers learnedly explain the transformation. *Neither Satan nor his followers*, they tell us, *can bear the daylight*.

It is *light*, then, that drives away devils, wizards, and witches. Little did those who said this know how truly they spoke. It is, in very truth, the light of a purer religion and of a more genuine science that has dispelled the night-mare of the middle-ages.

The two great causes which worked a deep change in the general state of the intellect, and thereby brought about the irretrievable decadence of belief in the devil, were the indirect influence of the Reformation, and the progress of science. It may seem surprising that we mention the Reformation here. The sixteenth century reformers in no sense opposed faith in the devil. Luther held to it closely; and so did most of his friends. It was owing to a certain coolness of intellect, to a distrust of whatever gave too free play to the imagination, that Calvin was always very cautious in speaking of a subject which turned the best heads; but he did not the less share the common notions of Satan and his power; and he asserted them more than once. It was an indirect, but not on that account a less cogent, influence to which we refer. What, among the nations who embraced the Reformation, struck the first blow, and a very telling one, at his infernal majesty, was, that all fear of him was taken away by virtue of the newly proclaimed principles. The idea of the absolute authority of God, which was so all-absorbing among the Protestants of the seventeenth century,—that idea which they pushed to the paradox of predestination,—quickly led them to regard Satan as a mere instrument of the divine will, and his doings as simply the means it pleased God to use in accomplishing his hidden designs. The Christian's faith enabled him to despise the rebel angel, who was powerless to harm the elect. We know what sort of reception he had when he paid Luther a visit at Wartburg. The simplification of the ritual, and the discredit of the supernatural power that had been attributed to the clergy, tended greatly to free the minds of the simple from the weary incubus. Exorcisms, whether at baptism, or in supposed cases of demoniacal possession, were done away with; those performances, that so terrified the imagination, in which the priest, flourishing his holy-water brush, attacked the devil with dashes of water, repaid by the evil one in frightful blasphemies, were at an end. People ceased to believe in *incubi* and *succubœ*. If, here and there, a person was thought to be possessed, prayer and moral exhortations were the only remedies employed; and ere long it became a very rare thing to hear demoniacs spoken of among Protestant peoples. The idea that the Bible miracles were the only true ones, illogical as it was, led people to live on from day to day without fearing or expecting any more to occur. The devil's miracles were the first to lose their credit when the decline of belief in the supernatural began. Thus Satan lapses into just what he was in the first century, or even to something less, a tempting, invisible, impalpable spirit, whose suggestions must be resisted, and from whom regeneration alone delivers us, and that surely. Even his old part in the drama of the redemption is no longer conceded to him. All now is transacted immediately between the faithful and his God. For it is now God, and no longer Satan, who is held to take the ransom offered by Jesus for the deliverance of sinners. In a word, without as yet thinking of denying Satan's existence and power, the Reformation, while still making great use of his name in popular teaching and preaching, by slow degrees dismisses him to an abstract, ideal sphere, without any clear connection with everyday life. Had he been looked upon simply as a convenient personification of the power of moral evil in the world, Protestant piety would have been but little affected.* French catholicism in its palmiest period, the seventeenth century, while influenced much more than is generally supposed by the Reformation, presents a very similar character. With what moderation do its most illustrious representative men, Bossuet, Fénelon, and even such preachers as Bourdaloue, treat this part of Catholic doctrine! Good taste takes with them the place of rationalism; and who, after reading their works, wonders that a Louis Quatorze, scant as was his tenderness in dealing with religious questions, could show himself sceptical in the matter of witchcraft, and less superstitious than the Parliament of Rouen?

Even in ages of the darkest ignorance, there were disbelievers in witches and wizards. The Lombard law, by a remarkable exception, forbade the prosecution of *masks*, as sorcerers were called in Italy. A king of Hungary of the eleventh century forbade mention to be

---

* The confirmation of what we advance here may be found in two facts, which are equally well-known though differing in character, namely, the conduct of the Protestant physician Duncan in the case of Urbain Grandier, and the poetical transformation of Satan under the pen of Milton in the midst of rigorous orthodoxy.

made of them, for the simple reason that they did not exist. Agobard, Archbishop of Lyons, classed belief in *sabbaths* among the absurdities bequeathed by paganism to the ignorant. The *Malleus Maleficarum* certainly had in view opponents who denied not only witchcraft, but also the intervention of the devil in human concerns, seeing that it insisted upon both in laboured scholastic arguments. At the time when trials for *leagues* with the devil were in full vogue, there was a brave Jesuit named Spee, whose humane feelings got the better of the spirit of his order. While engaged in the charge of souls in Franconia, it was his duty to accompany to the stake, during a few years, more than two hundred persons convicted of witchcraft. One day the Archbishop of Mayence, Philip of Schoenborn, asked him why he, a young man of scarcely thirty, had grey hair already. "Through grief," he replied, "for the many wizards I have had to prepare for death, no one of whom was guilty." It was he who wrote a *Cautio Criminalis*, printed under his name in 1631, and which, without denying witchcraft, or even the lawfulness of the penalties directed against it, entreats inquisitors and magistrates to increase their precautions against condemning so many innocents to capital punishment. Before Spee's time, a Protestant physician attached to the person of Duke William of Cleves had written in the same strain a book of considerable learning for the age, the fruit of distant voyages and numerous observations, in which, while he admitted the reality of magic, he denied witchcraft properly so called, and sharply charged the clergy with keeping alive popular superstitions, and making good folk believe that the troubles they could not help them through were the work of sorcerers who had sold themselves to the devil. It required no little courage to speak out thus in those days. To take the part of wizards was to expose one's-self to the charge of witchcraft; and in these sad annals examples are not rare of judges and priests who, victims of their humanity or their justice, were sentenced and burned with those whom they had sought to save. The French physician Gabriel Naude undertook the same treatment of the question in his *Apology for Men accused of Magic* (1669). But the causes the slow influence of which we have described had not yet so far transformed men's minds that they were able to emancipate themselves from the devil. A total demolition of the edifice was necessary on the one hand, and, on the other, a religious justification of this destruction. Here, as elsewhere, progress could only go on effectively upon the condition that religious sanction was blended with purely rational arguments. This law of human progress verifies itself in all times and with regard to all questions. If it is resisted, public opinion divides itself into two camps, which mutually hold one another in check; frowning at each other, without advancing a step. What had come through the Church, must pass away through the Church. The honour of striking a decisive blow at the superstition we are examining is due to the Dutch pastor Balthazar Bekker, who appeared in the lists, not only in the name of good sense and humanity, but as a theologian, and published his famous work, entitled, *The Enchanted World* (1691-1693). Four thousand copies exhausted in two months, the rapid translation of this thick book into all the languages of Europe, and the hot controversies it excited, all of which it has survived, suffice to show what a mark the work made upon the age.

It is quite true that the demonstrations of the Dutch theologian would not have like value in our eyes. Not yet venturing, for instance, to emancipate himself from the Scriptures, which he regarded as of infallible authority, he twists and turns the text in such a manner as to pare away the doctrine of a personal devil who busies himself with the actions and thoughts of men. He succeeds, however, in drawing attention to many details, not hitherto noticed, which go to prove that the

Scriptural teaching about the devil is neither definite, nor harmonious, nor in conformity with the opinions of the middle ages. He subjects to a pitiless criticism all the threadbare arguments that, on the ground of experience, had been used to uphold popular prejudice. His discussion of the trial of Urbain Grandier and the Ursulines of Loudun, which was still within every one's memory, must have greatly struck his readers. A fact like this, that could be analysed with the documents in one's hands, threw a clear light upon a heap of other more obscure cases of an older date, which had been constantly appealed to by the partisans of the devil. For the first time, too, universal history was laid under contribution to show that belief in devils established an incontestable relationship between the polytheistic and Christian faiths. The whole spirit of the book is summed up in the aphorisms with which it ends:— "There is no witchcraft where there is no faith in it; do not believe in it, and it will cease to be. . . . Get rid of all these silly old-wives' fables, and exercise yourselves in godliness." Here was true prophecy; but it was not given to the author to see it fulfilled. To making light of Satan he added the offence, a very grave one in the eyes of Dutch orthodoxy, of being a zealous Cartesian. He was deprived of his living by a synod, and died soon afterwards. But the career of his book could not be checked; and it made its way well. From the date of its appearance, the cause of the devil may be considered as rejected by the tribunal of scientific theology. The progress of the human mind, and the knowledge of nature and modern philosophy, did the rest.

The spirit of science, as constituted since the time of Bacon and Descartes, no longer tolerates the hurried conclusions that so easily gained the assent of the ages in which imagination bore rule, and in which men's readiness to pronounce judgment upon obscure questions was proportioned to their ignorance. Experimental philosophy, the only true method, gives as much solidity to the theses it verifies, as it inspires distrust of whatever avoids the scope of examination. Beyond all doubt there are essential truths which we cannot subject to the test of experience; but these, to say the least, compensate us for that drawback by their close affinity with our nature, our life, and our conscience. If, for instance, it could be said that belief in the devil commended itself to us on account of its great moral usefulness, in that it improves those who share it, and elevates a man's character by making him more pure and brave and unselfish, then there would be good motives for trying to save it from the formidable attacks of modern reason. But the reverse is the case. Belief in the devil necessarily tends to blunt the sense of individual culpability. If I do wrong, not because I am bad, but because another, whose power is stronger than my own will, has driven me into wrong-doing, then my fault is certainly lessened, if not annulled. We have passed under review the wretched superstitions, the dangerous follies, and terrible crimes, which this belief so long inspired. But the disproof of witchcraft carries with it, some may urge, no disproof of the existence of a personal evil genius, against whom men must defend themselves, as against a foe who goes about perpetually seeking to lead them on to sin. But let such reflect whether witchcraft can be so easily severed from the principle of which it is the offspring. Once admit the devil, and wizards follow as a matter of course. If there is really a being of superhuman strength, who seeks, as it is said, to work our moral ruin, for his private satisfaction, is it not evident that, in order the better to accomplish his end, he will try to catch weak souls, by putting in their way the means of procuring what they desire? It is quite consistent that belief in the devil should have found its definite outcome in belief in sorcerers, and that this latter, having succumbed before experience, should have carried in its ruin the belief in the devil himself. If there is, in good sooth, a devil, then there are wizards; and since there are no such things as wizards, it is clear there is no devil. This is what the condensed good sense of the three last centuries authorises us to conclude; and this conclusion still awaits refutation.

The eighteenth century made the mistake of supposing that traditional beliefs could be destroyed by turning them into ridicule. When a belief that has for awhile been derided has deep roots in the human conscience, it easily survives the sarcasms of which it has been the object; and the time comes when those sarcasms no longer move laughter, for they chafe the innermost feelings of religious persons, and the good taste of the sensitive. But in the devil's case the laughter of the eighteenth century has remained victorious. The truth is, the devil *is* ridiculous. That being who is presented to us as so cunning, so malicious, so cleverly selfish, who strives unceasingly to carry on the troublesome business of corrupting men's souls, turns out to be very foolish. When, brought down from the heights where poetry and mystery have sometimes succeeded in placing him, he is subjected to close inspection and confronted with plain truth, Satan becomes a mere absurdity; and ever since this has been clearly seen it has become impossible to honour him by acknowledging his real existence.

We could have lengthened our retrospective study of the works which, during the eighteenth century, and even in our own times, have continued a controversy that will henceforward be aimless. Ever since a true knowledge of the constitution of the universe has dissipated the illusions which formed an indispensable frame to the picture of the Satan of olden time—a fixed dome above, an earth in the midst, and a hell under the earth, —ever since we have been compelled to see God's presence live and move in all things, there is no more room left in the world for the devil. Nothing could be more wearisome and puerile than the endeavours of certain reactionary theologians, in Germany and elsewhere, to restore a shadow of reality to the old phantom, while at the same time escaping the gross superstitions to which even these retrograde divines can no longer commit themselves. In vain is an attempt made to preserve for him something like an honourable position in some few dogmatic treatises, and in pietistic hymns. This, when not met by sheer indifference, does but annoy those of the clergy and laity who are pervaded by a healthy tone. By them Satan is still tolerated as an expression, a type, a symbol which the language of religion has sanctioned; and this is all. But to allow him any place in civil or domestic codes, to admit him into actual life,—this is now quite out of the question; *non possumus*.

But is there absolutely no good to be got out of this error of such long standing, which occupies so much space in the history of religions, and dates from their very sources? Must we admit that, in this particular, the human mind has for all these centuries been feeding upon what is absolutely false? This cannot be so. There must surely be something in human nature which has pleaded in its favour, and has maintained from generation to generation a faith which is contradicted by experience. I will not assert, with some who have thought upon the matter, that the explanation lies in the ease with which this doctrine of the devil solved the problem of the origin of evil; for the truth is, that it solved nothing. It carried into heaven the problem that seemed insoluble on earth. But what did this avail? The main stay of faith in the devil, or the one constituent of that faith, is the power of evil in and around us. I wonder at the singular tranquillity with which almost all our French philosophers face this question, or rather forget it, while they dilate in eloquent phrases upon free-will. Let us look at the facts as they really stand. The truth is, that the best among us is a long way behind the ideal that he sets before him; he is too weak to realise this ideal; and, if he is sincere, he acknowledges his shortcomings. The truth is, that our weak morality is too often at the mercy of those surgings within us of the "Old Adam,"—that animal, carnal man, we carry within us, which has so often given the lie to the proud *satisfacit* we bestow upon ourselves so complacently. Another truth is this, that we are at every moment carried into evil by the social influences that surround us, and against the mischievous and impulsive current of which few have energy enough victoriously to hold their own. We must not fall into the extreme of those theologians who have taught the total depravity of the human race, and with it a method of regeneration; as if even a miracle could regenerate a totally corrupted nature. Observation proves that we are selfish, but capable of loving; that we are naturally sensual, but not less naturally attracted by the splendour of the true and the good; that we are very imperfect, but still perfectible. The first condition of progress is to feel wherein we fail. This is why the "Kingdom of heaven" is promised to the "poor in spirit," to those, that is, who are conscious of their poverty. If we would so live as to satisfy our conscience, we must learn to repel victoriously those attacks with which selfish sensuality, flesh and blood, and worldly fascinations assail us. This is the devilish power from which we must set ourselves free. There is a sense in which we may say we are all of us more or less "possessed." The mistake lies in *personifying* this power of evil. When theists say there is a personal God, they do not ignore the faultiness of the notion of personality as derived from our own human nature; but as it is impossible for us to conceive any other mode of existence save personality and impersonality, and as God must possess all perfection, they declare,—lacking a better term,—that he is personal because he is perfect, and because impersonal perfection is a contradiction. Evil, on the other hand, which is the diametrical opposite of the perfect, is necessarily impersonal. Against its baneful seductions, against its ever direful sorcery, must we wrestle, so that our true human personality, our moral personality, may triumphantly disengage itself from the soil allotted for our growth. Upon this condition depends its attaining to the regions of pure and steadfast morality, where nought that has the likeness of Satan can hinder our ascent God-ward. This alone remains of the doctrine of the devil. But this alone concerns our moral health; and this must never be forgotten.

www.ingramcontent.com/pod-product-compliance
Lightning Source LLC
Chambersburg PA
CBHW020255090426
42735CB00010B/1928